Howell Book House

A Simon & Schuster Macmillan Company
1633 Broadway
New York, NY 10019

Macmillan Publishing books may be purchased for business or sales promotional use. For information please write: Special Markets Department, Macmillan Publishing USA, 1633 Broadway, New York, NY 10019.

Library of Congress Cataloging-in-Publication Data
Rach, Julie.
The conure: an owner's guide to a happy, healthy pet / Julie Rach.
p. cm.
ISBN 0-87605226-X

1. Conures.   I. Title.   II. Series.
SF473.C65R335   1998
636.6'865—dc21   98-6585
                    CIP

Manufactured in the United States of America
10 9 8 7 6 5 4 3 2 1

Series Director: Amanda Pisani
Series Assistant Director: Jennifer Liberts
Book Design by Michele Laseau
Cover Design by Iris Jeromnimon
Photography:
  Front and back covers by Eric Ilasenko
  Font cover inset by B. Everett Webb
  Joan Balzarini: 24, 30, 31, 47, 75, 77, 80, 111, 116, 119
  Michael DeFreitas: 40
  Eric Ilasenko: i, 2–3, 8, 13, 23, 25, 26, 27, 33, 36, 38–39, 46, 61, 70, 79, 84, 86, 90, 108, 122
  Kelli Cates: 105
  Sherry Lee Harris: 6, 14, 15, 16, 17, 19, 21, 29, 37, 42, 44, 48, 53, 57, 60, 64, 66, 69, 109, 113, 114
  David Shulman: 81
  John Tyson: 10, 18, 22, 50, 56, 73, 78, 118
  B. Everett Webb: 5, 7, 9, 12, 14, 17, 20, 21, 41, 43, 45, 51, 52, 58, 62, 63, 65, 68, 71, 72, 83, 87, 106–107, 110
Production Team: Clint Lahnen, Stepahnie Mohler, Angel Perez, Heather Pope, Dennis Sheehan, Terri Sheehan

The
Conure

An Owner's Guide To

A HAPPY HEALTHY PET

Howell Book House